Moosehead Lake Reflections

Blessing Book
Volume One

"Twinkle" Marie Porter-Manning

Matrika Press

Moosehead Lake Reflections
Copyright © "Twinkle" Marie Porter-Manning
July 2020

All Rights Reserved
including the right of reproduction,
copying, or storage in any form
or means, including electronic,
In Whole or Part,
without prior written
permission of the author.

ISBN: 978-1-946088-22-2

1. Journal 2. Self Care 3. Self-Exploration
4. Spirituality 5. Philosophy 6. Keepsake
7. Travel Journal 8. Title

Matrika Press

Matrika Press
P.O. Box 115
Rockwood, Maine 04478
Editor@MatrikaPress.com

www.MatrikaPress.com

Dedication

To our grandchildren
Kai, Zoey, Gabriel, Cayson, Lila & River

You bring such joy to our lives!

May the experiences and memories
you share of our family camp
be as sweet and as special as each of you.

May Moosehead Lake always be a source
of comfort and peace to you
and to our family for generations to come.

Introduction

Blessing Books are created by "Twinkle" Marie Porter-Manning and are a source of intentional inspiration to be used to record personal messages to the owner of the Blessing Book. These mementos and keepsakes can be used in rituals, celebrations and communions as well as for self-reflection and documentation of one's innermost thoughts, feelings and beliefs. At the heart of Blessing Books is the desire to share sentiments, messages and stories that we can draw upon as sources of comfort and a reminder that we are loved. This Blessing Book was created for self-exploration and contemplation.

How to Use the Moosehead Lake Reflections book:

This book is designed to be used as a self-led retreat that you guide yourself on. Each day select a word or phrase that is meaningful to you. Place the word or phrase at the top of selected page. Use the content space provided to describe its significance. The space is kept intentionally small so as to encourage ease of this daily writing. There are quotes and daily prompts to serve as guides. Writers can spin off of these prompts or take their daily entry in an entirely different direction. ***This Blessing Book is about YOU.*** It can be used in times of joy or in times of sorrow. It can be used to mark a milestone such as a significant birthday or important season of your life. It can be used to help you process a loss or transition in your life. It can be the place you affirm what is *next* for you as you cross a threshold and visualize your greatest intention for your life. It can be a book of prayers and poems you create. It can be a travel journal or place where you reflect on the experience of Moosehead Lake.

Moosehead Lake Reflections can also be filled out by you as a gift for another, or as a treasure to be placed in your family's library as a book filled with your own reflections, beliefs, hopes and dreams you wish to pass on to your family.

If you prefer pictures than words, you can also place a photo or art in the space provided and describe it with a single word that reflects the moment and your day's contemplation.

Wherever you are on your journey, may this Blessing Book serve you well.

For more resources and rituals to accompany this book, including Blessing Stones, visit: **MatrikaPress.com/Blessing-Books**

This Blessing Book belongs to:

_____

Occasion:

_____

Date:

_____

Moosehead Lake Reflections
Table of Contents

1. _____
2. _____
3. _____
4. _____
5. _____
6. _____
7. _____
8. _____
9. _____
10. _____
11. _____
12. _____
13. _____

14. _____
15. _____
16. _____
17. _____
18. _____
19. _____
20. _____
21. _____
22. _____
23. _____
24. _____
25. _____
26. _____
27. _____
28. _____
29. _____
30. _____
31. _____
32. _____
33. _____

34. _____

35. _____

Reflections
Thoughts for Contemplation by the Author
About the Publisher
About the Author
Other Works by this Author
Coming Soon
Other Books by Matrika Press
Featured Titles
Resources

*"Without reflection, we go blindly on our way,
creating more unintended consequences,
and failing to achieve anything useful."*

— Margaret J. Wheatley

What do you carry on your heart and mind?
What would you most like to take time to explore?
What intended outcome would you most like
to be made manifest in your life?

Date: _____

1.

*"Learning to hold our own lives
with a gentle compassion
is a key element in all
emotional healing
and spiritual awakening."*

— Tara Brach

Where do you need the most compassion in your life?
In what ways can you be more gentle with yourself?

Date: _____

*"I had nothing to offer anybody
except my own confusion."*

— Jack Kerouac

What would you like to have clarity about
in this present moment?

Date: _____

*"When you were born you cried
and the world rejoiced;
Live your life so that when you die
the world cries and you rejoice."*

— Navajo Proverb

What do you want people to know about you?
What do you most want to be remembered for?
What would make you truly happy?

Date: _____

"A miracle is not defined by an event.
A miracle is defined by gratitude."

— *Rev. Kate Braestrup*

Describe some miracles!

Date: _____

"Holding me like gravity are places that pull."

— Eddie Vedder

What places and people are you most drawn to?

Date: _____

"I don't have to go around trying to save everybody anymore; that's not my job."

— Jada Pinkett Smith

If you could choose to focus on just you,
on improving one thing in your life,
what would that be?

Date: _____

"If I wished to see a mountain or other scenery
under the most favorable auspices,
I would go to it in foul weather,
so as to be there when it cleared up;
we are then in the most suitable mood,
and nature is most fresh and inspiring.
There is no serenity so fair as that which is just
established in a tearful eye"

― Henry David Thoreau

The quiet after the storm can be the most revealing.
What have the aftermath of storms in your
life's journey revealed to you?

Date: _____

"Water does not resist.
Water flows.
When you plunge your hand into it,
all you feel is a caress.
Water is not a solid wall, it will not stop you.
But water always goes where it wants to go,
and nothing in the end can stand against it.
Water is patient.
Dripping water wears away a stone.
Remember that, my child.
Remember you are half water.
If you can't go through an obstacle, go around it.
Water does."

― Margaret Atwood

In what circumstance in your life
would you benefit from being like water?

Date: _____

"If we tend to the things that are important in life,
if we are right with those we love,
and behave in line with our faith,
our lives will not be cursed with
the aching throb of unfulfilled business.
Our words will always be sincere,
our embraces will be tight.
We will never wallow in the agony of
'I could have, I should have.'
We can sleep in a storm."

― Mitch Albom

The practice of *Living Life as a Prayer* teaches the cultivation of a lifestyle that reflects your values and principals and to model with your thoughts, words and actions, the manner you wish to experience life's journey.

How do you tend to the important things in life?

Date: _____

*"All the gifts we've been given to share
Have been with us since life's beginning
and we never noticed they were there.
We can balance at the brink of wisdom,
never recognizing we've arrived.
Loving spirits will live together,
we're all swimming to the other side."*

— *Pat Humphries*

What gifts do you recognize in yourself?
How do you share them with others?

Date: _____

"I wake up every morning believing today is going to be better than yesterday."

— *Will Smith*

What do you want to experience today?

Date: _____

*"My candle burns at both ends;
It will not last the night;
But, ah my foes, and oh, my friends—
It gives a lovely light!"*

— Edna St. Vincent Millay

What tasks or projects can you let go of
to create more time for
rest, relaxation and rejuvenation?

Date: _____

"Spend less time tearing yourself apart, worrying if you're good enough. You are good enough"

— Reese Witherspoon

What is the most amazing thing about you?

Date: _____

*"This weight's too much alone
Some days I can't hold it at all."*
— Jack Johnson

*"But just remember on the way home,
That you were never meant to feel alone."*
— John Mayer

Rev. Ian White Mayer's first and foremost solution to every challenge is: *"To Invite God In."* He says that, *"Once I've called myself to rest in the spiritual place, then the other solutions appear."*

Even in our loneliest moments, we do not have to feel alone. We can access that which we personally identify as Divine and call that in to accompany us.

What is your interpretation of God? Of The Holy?
Where do you draw your faith from?
What is Sacred to you?

Date: _____

*"My first lessons in spirituality and yoga
had nothing to do with a mat,
but everything to do with waking up."*

— Seane Corn

Describe a moment when you realized you were
waking up to new understandings about life
and about how to live it?

Date: _____

"The chances you take, the people you meet, the people you love, the faith that you have. That's what's going to define you."

— *Denzel Washington*

Look out across the lake, or into the woods, or up at the mountains, perhaps Kineo is before you. Breathe in (or envision) the fresh Maine air around you.

Now: Define yourself.

Date: _____

"Songs are about whatever you want them to be about. For me it might mean something completely different than what it means to you. So I'd say it's about whatever the listener thinks it's about."

— Norah Jones

Wherever you are in this place and time, what is its significance to you?

Date: _____

"Endings are beginnings if we allow them to be."

— *Laura Day*

What new beginning is available to you,
if you accept the ending of that which
you are holding on to?

Date: _____

*"Vision is the ability to talk about the future
with such clarity it is as if
we are talking about the past."*

— Simon Sinek

What wonderful things do you envision for your life?

Date: _____

*"There's too much confusion,
I can't get no relief."*

— Bob Dylan

What aspects of your life, or the world around you,
do you seek clarity about, and relief from?

Date: _____

"I speak no words of limitation."
— Rev. Dr. Della Reese Lett

"Show me how big your brave is."
— Sara Bareilles

What is your definition of "brave"?
What is the bravest thing you can do for yourself?

Date: _____

""There's a light, burning bright,
showing me the way;
But I know where I've been.

There's a cry in the distance;
It's a voice that comes from deep within.
There's a cry asking why,
I pray the answer's up ahead, yeah
'Cause I know where I've been"

□ Queen Latifah

Our pasts can be the single most destructive thing for our futures, if we let it define who we are today.
Release the burdens of the past.
Follow the light toward your future.
What do you see?

Date: _____

*"Happiness can be found,
even in the darkest of times,
if one only remembers
to turn on the light."*

—J.K. Rowling

What brings you the most happiness?

Date: _____

*"Life can only be understood backwards,
but it has to be lived forwards."*

— Søren Kierkegaard

What do you believe the purpose of life is?

Date: _____

*"Forget your perfect offering.
There is a crack in everything;
That's how the light gets in."*

— Leonard Cohen

What difficult experience has yielded beauty in your life?

Date: _____

"Always give back to the creator with happiness, kindness and love."

*— Bernadette Gahdele Rombough,
Dene Medicine Woman*

In what ways do you give back
to that which is most sacred to you?

Date: _____

*"Sit down beside us, Beloved, in the garden,
and let us rest against your knees, that we may
recount why we are thankful and how.
At the end of our days, may we be thankful
for all the chances to choose love and
to choose hope and to choose justice and to choose
generosity and to choose wonderment
and to choose joy."*

— *Rev. Naomi King*

What is your prayer for your life?
What is your prayer for humanity?
What are you thankful for?

Date: _____

"Make your heart like a lake, with a calm, still surface, and great depths of kindness."

— *Lao Tzu*

When are you most calm?
What spiritual practice allows you to be at peace?

Date: _____

"The ultimate touchstone of friendship is witness,
the privilege of having been seen by someone
and the equal privilege of being granted
the sight of the essence of another,
to have walked with them
and to have believed in them,
and sometimes just to have
accompanied them on a journey
impossible to accomplish alone."

— David Whyte

How have you experienced this depth of friendship?

Date: _____

"The heart is our main electrical power center. Producing 2.5 watts of power, it generates forty to sixty times more power than the brain. The heartbeat, which produces an electrical signal, can be measured at any point on the body..."

— Doc Lew Childre

With every beat of our heart we can focus our attention on benevolent thoughts and actions, and we can send this signal out to those around us, as well, for our heartbeat acts as a communication pathway inside our bodies, and also to the outer world.

Where, to what, and to whom do you most want to dedicate your heart's energy to?

Date: _____

"Because I have loved, I am changed;
Because I have loved,
I can see.
Because I have loved, I am changed;
Because I am loved,
I am free.
Where love has been, love will remain.

— Sheryl Crow

Where does love reside in your life?

Date: _____

"The greatness of a community is most accurately measured by the compassionate actions of its members."
— Coretta Scott King

"In Native American traditions, there is a saying that sums up the role of humanity, nature, and the divine quite well: 'It is a foolish tree whose branches fight among itself.'"
— Christopher Penczak

How do you demonstrate compassion?

Date: _____

*"The idealist most easily succumbs (to):
activism and overwork.*

*To allow oneself to be carried away
by a multitude of conflicting concerns,
to surrender to too many demands,
to commit oneself to too many projects,
to want to help everyone in everything…
…destroys our own inner capacity for peace."*

— *Thomas Merton*

If your life feels frenzied and out of control, if you are anxious that there is not enough 'time' in any given day, what are you willing to set boundaries on to ensure you can have peace in your heart, and peace in your mind?

Date: _____

*"When I breathe in, I breathe in peace.
When I breathe out, I breathe out love."*

— *Sarah Dan Jones*

Breathe in peace.
Breathe out love.
Again.
Again.
Again.

How do you feel?
What is 'next' for your life's journey?

Date: _____

Reflections

What additional discernments have come through to you during these Moosehead Lake Reflections?

Thoughts for Contemplation
Including musings, poetry, meditations, teachings and prayers.

Listen
Breathe in each morning the magick of Life;
Breathe out each evening deep gratitude for living.
And Listen to the Call of the Universe
in every interaction
in every curve in the road
in every commitment to task
in every covenant of relationship
in every whispered word
in every meditation
in every prayer
in every song
Listen.

May we enter the Holy Quiet:
That place of Being that is within us,
and through us, and beyond us.

Many spiritual practices turn our attention towards the infinite, which can help us see the larger picture of Oneness, yet it can sometimes also serve as a spiritual bypassing of sorts, which can become a habitual distraction, addictive in detaching (or hiding) rather than coping with what is present in our lives.

Bringing it to the finite perspective – which is truly what we have in each given moment – is not only more manageable, but also practical in a spiritual sense because it opens the door to deep gratitude for the life we have, even if we are struggling in the moment, we are present to it and able to do something about it.

May Love be the light
and Grace be the compass
that reveal the way forward.

Consider with me this:

There is a divine echo that whispers
within every heart.
Indeed, that every soul carries with it
the echo of a intrinsic intimacy.
An original echo that is brought fourth
through time from original source.
A primal source where we are all One.
And we carry the essence of this original echo
as a talisman of our divinity.

There exists a place in our hearts where intimacy has
no limit and love has no barrier.

When one listens to the Universe,
the Universe listens back.

Does time echo forward?
Or does it echo back?
It seems to me the latter.
But is it possible to track?
Coincidences coincide continually.
Yet are they purposeful perpetually?
It seems to me quite possibly.
But is this reality?

When the need for silence is great
Yet its soulful sound is filled instead
With errant thoughts granted unguarded audience by
Ego's solicitations to sadness,
Allow your heart to be occupied with
Hildegard's beseeching praise of the Divine;
Allow yourself to immerse in the space
Of such holy tenderness;
Within this musical embrace
You will find silence holds you.

Do you Pray?
I pray daily and throughout the day.
My life is a life of prayer.
My journey with prayer has been
an ever evolving one.
At present prayer to me is surrender and gratitude.
The first, surrender, is in communion with,
and experience of, the Holy.
The second, deep gratitude for the Holy and the
many gifts in my life. The outward appearance of
such prayers can be formal or spontaneous:
intentional moments of stillness and silence, visualization, or active with writing, creating art, chanting
or singing or drawing down the moon, walking in
the woods and along the river, speaking out loud my
heart's desires or giving a blessing, it is the lullabies
with my child each night….Prayer is even found in
doing the dishes at my kitchen sink,
and dancing in my living room.

May you live Life as a Prayer.

I believe that prayer can be as diverse as that which
we call Holy and can be made manifest through
words, thoughts and deeds, such as daily acts of grace
and gratitude.

I turn to prayer in gratitude and also in surrender
when circumstances are beyond my control. Sometimes my prayers manifest in writings and visualizations; oftentimes the simple act of touching my hand
to my heart and humming (kind of like the Om)
places me in conscious union with the divine.

My guess is, that we each have something that
we feel is Holy. And I urge you to turn to that first.
When feeling vulnerable, when feeling scared,
when feeling like you are just not quite
feeling like yourself,
Turn to that which you identify as Holy,
identify as Sacred.

When we live life as a prayer,
our reactions to situations and to people
become subtle,
even unconscious,
manifestations of the prayer
we bring in to the world.

We begin to recognize the beauty blossoming
in our own hearts and minds.
And as that beauty blossoms,
we recognize with clarity
the callings of our heart;
the *callings* from God.
And it is this,
hearing and answering our callings,
which transforms our otherwise transient lives
into union with the Divine.
This union becomes evident in the transfiguration
of our thoughts,
and our emotions.
And when this happens
we no longer need to clench when faced with
challenging situations
or difficult people.

What if hospitality
was the pillar of our Faith?

If coming together
created sanctuary?

If sharing Joys and Sorrows
was the path to enlightenment?

What if our sacred texts
were our sermons, poems and songs?

If our principles
were our doctrines?

If our covenant
was the Hope that binds us?

Indeed,
What if compassion presided
over our thoughts and our deeds?

Life is center-oriented.

A supportive force, designed
to bring us naturally into alignment.
The catch?
It requires our active participation.
In return, it gives us the needed gravitational pull to center.
It does not require us to reject any part of our selves.
Yet is does demand we have a clear center to orient us.
With that in balance, we can be confident that
we can align all parts as we hold close to our center
with seemingly effortless grace.

The sustainability of the peace, joy, and purpose
we discover in our hearts
is strengthened (and weakened)
by the people and communities we choose
to surround ourselves with.

In myriad ways, we connect and affect.

Whatever is inside of us continually flows outward;
Whatever is outside us continually flows inward.

If life on the outside is presenting
things to be grateful for,
gather the gratitude for those
into your Heart's storehouse.

If life on the outside is presenting things
that cause you to feel fear or sadness,
reach into your heart and find
the place where your love
and your gratitude
and your peace
and peace of mind
resides
and bring that forward.

Because the world needs it.
You need it.

To have resolve is to be gifted
unyielding firmness or endurance.

To practice resolve is to act
with robust commitment that is
made possible by a strong,
healthy, dynamic faith.

May it be known
That I retrieve all I am
To do all I am meant to.
From this moment on.
So mote it be.

May your life be filled with a kaleidoscope of color
and beauty and joy.

May we be like the trees
and transform our world
with every breath.

May deep listening begin to take place from every
corner of each controversial discussion.
Deep listening without accusations.
Deep listening with the goal
of understanding each other.
May we remember we are a people of Love.

May we understand that
we are capable of being loved,
no matter what wounds we still carry,
no matter what mistakes we still make.
May we know that
we are capable of loving generously,
even beyond our wildest imaginations.
May we see
beyond the shadow and into the Soul.
Amen and Blessed Be.

As a society, we treat Time as if we have
a surplus attached to a lavish line of credit
and syphon it into a plethoric gluttony
of distractions.
We are either numb to,
or feel the pressing weight of,
the tedious excess expected of our Time.
Time, a commodity
impossible to trade for its actual value.
Time, a trust fund
we cannot save for a rainy day.
Time, a gift
that comes with freedom of will.
Time, gaining equity
only in legacy.

How important it is to make every moment count.

This Dance of ours, Life's Journey,
consists of
Time and the Choices we make.
Choosing Directions
for our life's course
and
Perpetual Migrations
to live in to those choices.
Some directions are complicated.
Some Migrations are short distances.
We carry from these our memories
and the ramifications
of Time and of Choices.

Every moment alive,
we get to choose
where our Time reserve goes,
how we spend it,
and who we allow to draw from it.

Perhaps our greatest responsibility
is truly to be mindful of our Time.

Instead of one call to action after another,
how about a call to rest,
to be still,
to go within,
to look each other in the eyes,
to hold each other,
to be with one another.

What I am suggesting,
What I'm imploring,
And what I am asking...
...is for you to give yourself permission to rest.

Relax.
Unclench.
Breathe.

Sacred.
Benevolent.
Loving.

Moving forward is necessary;
"moving on" is impossible.

Our loved-one's death was more than a moment;
their life is more than a memory.

Their existence is ever-present
as they shape our lives even now.

The Afterward is a place we all must travel to
on our paths towards wholeness and healing.
The Afterward in not meant to be permanent
Accept that there is more than the Afterward.
There is the Next.
There is Life.
There is Now.

Because we belong together,
we are called to exercise compassion
towards each other,
and, towards ourselves.

It is the act of compassion that awakens us
to bring forth our best gifts to our community.

It is the act of self-compassion that emboldens us
to be brave,
and by 'be brave'
I mean it is self-compassion that allows us
to be vulnerable enough
to give over our burdens and our sorrows
into the tender loving care of our community.

Shared vulnerability,
sharing our most joyful experiences,
along with our sorrows,
this is what builds strength.

Strength in our community.
Strength in each of us.

May we build such Beloved Communities.

Beyond an altruistic "unconditional love"
is the concept of a trusted-love,
an "undoubted love."
The kind of love that is mutually intentional,
mutually experienced.
May we know how to love and be loved in return.

To attain spiritual enlightenment,
spiritual sophistication, spiritual maturity,
requires the full acceptance,
welcoming and claiming of the human experience.
This unequivocally means the integration
of our sexuality into our spirituality.
We are happier, healthier, body, mind and spirit
when we embrace and embody our sacred sexuality.
As such, the energy flowing outward from us
into our relationships and communities
reflects this well-being.

Sabbatical Thinking

If in the fabric of our human lives
we built our organizations,
our communities,
our nations,
with the sentiment that we are indeed One,
we would begin to weave together lifestyles,
and cultures,
and ways of being that support,
and lift up,
nurture and nourish such Oneness.
In such a society,
we would install extended times of rest
and enrichment and sabbatical and retreat.
For everyone.

Love the Land You're With.

Doing so creates an embodied relationship with Nature.

If you live near the ocean, you can connect with the resonance of Her rhythms, finding both strength and healing there. Immerse in her wisdom. Enjoy the Oceans' sandy beaches and weathered cliffs. They provide long moments of reflection and inspiration. The metaphysical aspects of our souls open in Her presence. Unimaginable horizons open to us as the inescapable reality of the vastness of Life is before us each day and every night.

Inland you can find lakes and mountains that ground us in this place in Time, while providing us insights on the legacies of those who came before us, and the ones that will follow. In their stillness and aliveness, the mountains, the lake, the land and trees and fields that surround us guide us to embrace a deeper connection with Earth and with Spirit. If you live inward, both literally and symbolically, you can experience an ever-evolving transformation and awakening. Inland Life provides us with the opportunity to grow and to harvest as we work with the soil of the Land. Many find that inland they are nurtured and more nurturing.

Restoring Harmony

When what we recognize as disharmony
materializes, especially when the disharmony creates
physical isolation from the people we love,
the places we like to spend time,
and the routines and rituals we've organized
our lives around, we can feel deeply disconnected.
Disconnected from that which we hold dear.
Disconnected from our own self assuredness
and self awareness.
Disconnected from where we draw our faith.
This disconnected feeling feels like chaos to us.
Disrupting the harmony we recognize as holy.
As sacred. As safe.
Yet if we can still the emotional storm that is rising.
If we can locate calmness in our bodies, in our beings,
we can restore the harmony.
As we cultivate this practice of weaving harmony from
within the chaos, we become the conductor in the
symphony of our emotions. This does not mean the
chaos disappears entirely. Nor that we receive answers
we like to all the things we have questions about.
But it makes space, intentionally so, for us to navigate
effectively within what Life has presented us with.

The Peaceable People

Who were the peaceable people?
The tribe whose culture never in all their history
oppressed another tribe?
Nor oppressed anyone within their own tribe?
What covenants did they create to facilitate peace-
ableness?
What race were they?
What color were they?
Which genders were they?
Which lands were sacred to them?
Which deities did they call their own?
Where did they come from?
Where did they go?
Where did they reside when the world was coming
apart at the seams?
Where are they now?
Why did their peaceable reign end?
How can we achieve such peaceableness again?
When do we begin?

About the Publisher

Matrika Press is an independent publishing house dedicated to publishing works in alignment with liberal religious values, principles, spiritualities and philosophies. Matrika Press is connected with The Church of Kineo, an emerging ministry in Rockwood, Maine. Its current fiscal sponsor is Unitarian Universalist Women and Religion, a 501c3 organization.

Matrika Press publishes anthologies, memoirs, poetry, prayer and ritual manuscripts, and other books to bring meaning and transformation to the world. A primary goal of Matrika Press is to publish stories and works that would otherwise remain untold. We also resurrect out-of-print manuscripts to ensure our historical works remain accessible.

Why the name "Matrika"?
It is said that Matrika is the intrinsic energy or sound vibration of the 50 letters of the Sanskrit alphabet called "the mothers of creation." The Goddess Kali Ma used the letters to form words, and from the words formed all things. This aligns with scriptures that assert "in the beginning was the Word," and in other sacred texts that affirm people of all backgrounds and faiths agree: Words are powerful. More than that: Their vibrations are creative forces; they bring all things into being.

Matrika Press titles are automatically made available to tens of thousands of retailers, libraries, schools, and other distribution and fulfillment partners, including Amazon, Barnes & Noble, Chapters/Indigo (Canada), and other well-known book retailers and wholesalers across North America, and in the United Kingdom, Europe, Australia and New Zealand and other Global partners.

For more information, visit:

www.MatrikaPress.com

About the Author

Rev. "Twinkle" Marie Porter-Manning is an interfaith minister, skilled ritualist and liturgist who has been leading workshops and seminars in the secular and spiritual worlds for more than two decades. She actively develops and leads programs that nourish spirituality. Her rituals, reflections and poetry have been included internationally in all manner of worship services and publications.

The series of *Blessing Books* is the newest of her publishing endeavors. Other published works include the *Women of Spirit* anthology series, *Intentional Visualization, Be Like the Trees, Restore Us to Memory*, and the *Pulpit of Peace* collection. Upcoming works include the *Sophia* anthologies series, *Anam Ċara and The Divine Echo,* and *Living Life as a Prayer*.

Her community ministry has long been known affectionately as *Twinkle's Place,* where she hosts a variety of retreats and spiritual programs. She shares a home in Rockwood, Maine with her husband and their youngest son.

www.MatrikaPress.com/twinkle-marie-manning
www.MooseheadLakeRetreats.org
www.TwinklesPlace.org

Other Works by this Author

www.MatrikaPress.com/women-of-spirit

Women of Spirit, Exploring Sacred Paths of Wisdom Keepers is a compilation of women sojourners, sages, mystics, witches, shaman, medicine women, ministers, philosophers, therapists, life coaches, yogis, and more.
Their journeys.
Their stories.
Their teachings and practices.
Essays, Poetry, Art, Rituals and Prayers.
This anthology is full of useful tools and powerful messages for everyone who is on a spiritual journey to embrace and enjoy. Beloved Contributors include:

- *Anna Huckabee Tull*
- *Bernadette Rombough*
- *Deb Elbaum* • *Deborah Diamond*
- *Debra Wilson Guttas* • *Grace Ventura*
- *Janeen Barnett* • *JoAnne Bassett*
- *Judy Ann Foster* • *Julie Matheson*
- *Kate Early* • *Kate Kavanagh*
- *Katherine Glass* • *Kris Oster*
- *Lea M. Hill* • *Meghan Gilroy*
- *Morwen Two Feathers* • *Rustie MacDonald*
- *Shamanaca* • *Sharon Hinckley*
- *Shawna Allard* • *Shiloh Sophia*
- *Susan Feathers* • *Tiffany Cano*
- *Tory Londergan*
- *"Twinkle" Marie Porter-Manning*
- *Tziporah Kingsbury* • *Valerie Sorrentino*

Pulpit of Peace: *Inspirational Quotes from a Prophetic Ministry*

This book features excerpts from Rev. Dr. "Twinkle" Marie Porter-Manning's sermons, as well as glimpses of her poetry, meditations, rituals and reflections. Common themes of her ministry and writings found in this book include: Building The Beloved Community; Möbius Life; Explorations of Divinity; Living Life as a Prayer.

Pulpit of Peace is part of the *a Pocketful Book Series.*

Be Like the Trees *(a Sermon in My Pocket)* speaks candidly about tragedy, grief, and challenges faced in daily life. Rev. Dr. "Twinkle" Marie Porter-Manning's words weave together a beautiful collage of insights and inspirations as she directs us towards the interconnectedness and magic of our human existence.

Coming Soon...

Living Life as a Prayer

The concurrent and foundational themes in the teachings of Living Life as a Prayer are of creating The Beloved Community, Möbius principles, Sabbatical lifestyles and connecting intentionally with that which we identify as Holy.

www.MatrikaPress.com

Coming Soon to the "a Sermon in My Pocket" series:

Restore Us to Memory
explores remembering (and reclaiming) who we are and offers encouragement to live our lives in such a way that we will be remembered how, and as who, we want to be remembered as.

Anam Ċara and The Divine Echo
centers a mystical aspect of belonging, and practical ways to demonstrate such belonging in our lives.

Other Books by Matrika Press

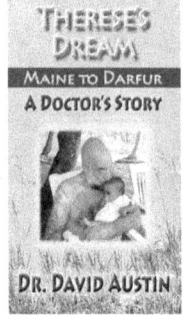

www.MatrikaPress.com

Featured Titles

The Circle Model of Shared Leadership by Elizabeth Fisher is a concrete group facilitation process that balances achieving tasks with emotional bonding. By using this book you will:
- Learn ways to bring a collection of individuals together, in a committee, board, or activist project, uniting each one's efforts which are equally valued.
- Develop skills critical to honing participatory decision-making and supporting the soul of the group, which must be kept strong if the group is to accomplish its goals.
- Discover important principles, practices and tools that support effective collaboration within and among all the levels of organizations.

www.MatrikaPress.com/the-circle-model

Sue Roy Humphries' historic aggregation work featuring behind-the-scenes documentation of sci-fi and horror classics in theatrical make-up effects has been all but hidden from the world for decades. Originally published in 1980, **Making a Monster** has been long out of print.

Matrika Press is delighted to revive this manuscript on its 40th Anniversary in response to those seeking a comprehensive montage of this highly creative aspect of filmmaking.

Making a Monster reveals the artistic secrets of your favorite vintage fantasy films. This book is filled with detailed accounts of the early era of makeup processes and ingenious solutions to the challenges of pre-CGI Visual FX.

While the manuscript reveals the trade and techniques of transforming some of Hollywood's most beautiful and beloved icons into infamous villains and fantastical creatures, its content also lends a lens unto the human psyche, including that of choosing what to believe in. Said another way, choosing One's Faith.

www.MatrikaPress.com/making-a-monster

Surf & Earth Designs

Joscelyne Drew is an award winning artist and one of the pioneers in ocean and abstract themed resin art. Her years of experience developing a distinctive beautiful technique and formulas have achieved a look that is like no other. Her work has been included in shows spanning from the Florida keys to Maine.

Joscelyne's abstract and contemporary nautical, reef and earth elements inspired resin art is also ideal for tables and bar-tops.

Commissions and custom orders of any size are welcomed!

www.facebook.com/SurfandEarthDesigns

www.ingramcontent.com/pod-product-compliance
Lightning Source LLC
Chambersburg PA
CBHW081751100526
44592CB00015B/2389